First World War
and Army of Occupation
War Diary
France, Belgium and Germany

14 DIVISION
41 Infantry Brigade,
Brigade Light Trench Mortar Battery
1 January 1919 - 17 February 1919

WO95/1896/6

The Naval & Military Press Ltd
www.nmarchive.com
Published in association with The National Archives

Published by

The Naval & Military Press Ltd

Unit 10 Ridgewood Industrial Park,

Uckfield, East Sussex,

TN22 5QE England

Tel: +44 (0) 1825 749494

www.naval-military-press.com

www.nmarchive.com

This diary has been reprinted in facsimile from the original. Any imperfections are inevitably reproduced and the quality may fall short of modern type and cartographic standards.

© **Crown Copyright**
Images reproduced by permission of The National Archives, London, England, 2015.

Contents

Document type	Place/Title	Date From	Date To
Heading	1896/6		
Heading	14th Division 41st Infy Bde 41st Lt Trench Mortar Bty Jan-Feb 1919		
Heading	War Diary Of 41st Light Trench Mortar Battery. From 1st January, 1919. To 31st January, 1919 Volume VIII.		
War Diary	Bondues	01/01/1919	04/01/1919
War Diary	Tourcoing	05/01/1919	31/01/1919
Miscellaneous	41st Trench Mortar Battery Nominal Roll Of Officers & O.Rs On Establishment	03/11/1918	03/11/1918
Miscellaneous	41st L.T.M.B Disposition Of Personnel		
Heading	War Diary Of 41st Light Trench Mortar Battery From 1st February 1919 To 28th February 1919 Volume IX		
War Diary	Tourcoing	01/02/1919	17/02/1919

1981

14TH DIVISION
41ST INFY BDE

41ST LT TRENCH MORTAR BTY
JAN - FEB 1919

C O N F I D E N T I A L.

W A R D I A R Y

- of -

41st LIGHT TRENCH MORTAR BATTERY.

From: 1st January, 1919.
To; 31st January, 1919.

VOLUME VIII.

Army Form C. 2118.

41st L.T.M.B.

WAR DIARY
or
INTELLIGENCE SUMMARY. JANUARY 1919.
(Erase heading not required.)

Place	Date	Hour	Summary of Events and Information	Remarks and references to Appendices
BONDUES.	1st		Recreation Training.	null
"	2nd		"	null
"	3rd		" No 86036 Rfn Box 33rd L.R.B. on leave to U.K.	null
"	4th		BATTERY move to TOURCOING. No 86030S Rfn Barton returned from Hospital.	null
TOURCOING.	5th		Recreation Training. No 104309 Sgt Hopkins 29.D.L.I. returned from leave to U.K.	null
"	6th		" 2nd Lieut R.V. Atkins 29th D.L.I. on leave to U.K.	null
"	7th		" off Strength to UK for Demobilisation No 10104 Pte Griffiths 29.D.L.I.	null
"	8th		" Pte No 62423. Lamb. J. 13th Y.L. to Hospital.	null
"	9th		" No 57614 Pte Childs. S. + No 57906 Rfn Lynch to Hospital	null
"	10th		" No 62239 Pte French J. to Hospital. 135 Y.L. 2nd Lieut AV Booth returned	null
"	11th		from leave to U.K.	null
"	12th		Recreation Training.	null
"	13th		Unfollowing off Strength, to U.K. for Demobilisation. 18th Y.L. No 6961 Pte Brewin H. +No 53604 Pte Ash. S. On leave to U.K., Capt E.K.B. Peck ME + No 4143 Rfn Oates	null
	13th		Recreation Training. to Hospital No 20969b. Cpl McLean 18th Y.L.	null
	14th		The following returned to duty from Hospital. Cpl McLean Pte Francis	null

WAR DIARY

N° 25.T.M.B.

Army Form C. 2118.

INTELLIGENCE SUMMARY. JANUARY 1919.

(Erase heading not required.)

Place	Date	Hour	Summary of Events and Information	Remarks and references to Appendices
TOUR COING.	15th		Recreation Training.	25 MB
	16th		" to Hospital N° 101698 Pte Bolan. J. 29th D.L.I.	25 MB
	17th		Returned from leave to UK 2nd Lieut J.A. Askin 18th Y.L. from Hospital N° 53604 Pte Child 18th Y.L.	25 MB
	18th		" Unit. N° 62541 Pte Wotsey 18th Y.L. Demobilized N° 101664 Pte Collins 29th D.L.I.	25 MB
	19th		Admitted to Hospital N° 101660 Pte Hoblin 29th D.L.I.	25 MB
	20th		Demobilized N° 860307 Rfn Findlay 38th L.R.B. from Hospital Pte Gower 18th Y.L.	25 MB
	21st		" N° 860305 Rfn Barton 38th L.R.B. from Hospital Pte Bolan 29th D.L.I. " " to Hospital.	25 MB
	22nd		from Hospital N° 61492 Pte Lant. 18th Y.L.	25 MB
	23rd		Recreation Training.	25 MB
	24th		"	25 MB
	25th		" Demobilized N° 101309 Cpl Hopkin 29th D.L.I.	25 MB
	26th		"	25 MB
	27th		On leave to U.K. N° 53685 Pte Harper F. 18th Y.L. From Hospital Pte Lynch 38th L.R.B.	25 MB
	28th		Recreation Training.	25 MB
	29th		Demobilized 18th Y.L. N° 62452 Pte Slack +N° 6202? Pte Chapman. From Hospital Pte James 25 MB	
	30th 31st		Recreation Training.	25 MB

Jun Deen Capt
OC N° 25 T.M.B.

3/11/18.

41ST TRENCH MORTAR BATTERY.

Nominal Roll of Officers & O.Rs on Establishment.

Captain E.K.B. PECK, 18th Y & L Regt.   Commanding.
2/Lieut. A.V. DOOMER, 3rd Essex Regt.
2/Lieut. R.V. ATKINS, 20th Durham L.I.
2/Lieut. J.A. ASKIN, 18th Y & L Regt.

238087	L/Sgt.	Beer,	H.	18th York & Lancs Regt.
209696	Cpl.	McLean,	W.S.	"
53604	Pte.	Ash,	T.	"
62028	"	Chapman,	C.H.	"
33800	"	Hilliard,	W.	"
238096	"	Pavelin,	F.	"
208696	"	Dempsey,	C.	"
62175	"	Watkinson,	C.	"
61961	"	Brewin,	H.	"
53614	"	Childs	S.	"
53683	"	Harper,	F.	"
200624	L/Cpl.	Reaney,	S.	"
208605	Pte.	Jones,	H.	"
101634	Sgt.	Scotland,	D.	29th Durham L.I.
101669	A/L/C.	Davies,	H.R.	"
101664	Pte.	Collins,	D.	"
101667	"	Ferriss,	H.W.	"
101660	"	Holden,	G.	"
101666	"	Procter,	W.	"
101729	"	Fox,	S.	"
101592	"	Hammond,	F.V.	"
101500	L/Cpl.	Hopkins,	M.	"
101665	Pte.	Hammond,	J.L	"
104232	"	Reeves,	W.	"
205437	L/Cpl.	Nixon,	J.	"
85529	Pte.	Tracey,	J.	"
100069	"	Marriott,	F.	"
85617	"	Barrett,	G.H.	"
101698	"	Bolan,	J.	"
104186	"	Myhill,	W.	"
879087	L/Sgt.	Erskine,	J.W.	23rd London
879059	A/L/Cpl.	Brook,	W.H.	"
860305	Pte.	Barton,	G.	"
879065	"	Domes,	A.S.	"
860307	"	Findlay,	F.C.	"
879062	"	Hewlett,	G.J.	"
879068	"	Lynch,	J.M.	"
879069	"	O'Brien,	T.	"
860306	"	Box,	P.G.	"
879056	L/Cpl	Sadler,	J.	"
860818	"	Hall,	E.	"
860872	"	Pritchard,	S.	"
860432	"	Rutter,	L.V.	"
860175	"	Green,	H.	"
861092	"	Wilson,	H.	"
860632	"	Robinson,	R.	"

Attached personnel.

62452	Pte.	Black,	J.H.	18th York & Lancs
62341	"	Warden,	A.	"
62605	"	Shaw,	H.	"
62239	"	France,	F.	"
62493	"	Lamb,	F.	"
61979	"	Weber,	W.	"
101926	"	Goldsmith,	E.	29th Durham L.I.
101984	"	Sunderland,	C.	"
294032	"	Leggett,	H.D.	"
860782	Rfn.	Edwards,	J.F.	23rd London Regt.
860607	"	Neale,	E.	"
41434	"	Oates,	J.	29. D.L.I.

41ST L.T.M.B

DISPOSITION OF PERSONNEL

2/Lt. R. Vestkins. 29th D.L.I.
101634 Sgt Scotland D   ⎫
104309 A/Cpl Hopkinson   ⎪
101729 Pte Fox. S   ⎪
101666 "   Proctor. W   ⎪
101665 "   Hammond. J.H   ⎪
101926 "   Griffiths E   ⎬ 29th. D.L.I
101984 "   Sunderland G   ⎪   Section.
101660 "   Holden. G   ⎪
101592 "   Hammond. J.V   ⎪
104232 "   Reeves. W   ⎪
101648 "   Bolam. J   ⎪
104186 "   Ayhill. W   ⎭

2/Lt. A.V. Booker 3rd Essex Rgt.
87905? L/Cpl Sadler. G 33rd London Rgt. R.B. ⎫
879059 A/ Brook. W.H   "   ⎪
879065 Pte Bence. E.S A/Cpl   "   ⎪
879064 Rfn O'Brien J   " Hosp   ⎪
860306 "   Box. P.S   " leave   ⎬ 33rd London Rgt. R.B
879052 "   Hewlett G   "   ⎪   Section.
860432 "   Rutter L.G   "   ⎪
860872 "   Ritchmond   "   ⎪
860818 "   Hall. E   "   41434 Rfn Oates J 33 L.R.B
860305 "   Barton G   Hosp   "   ⎪
860632 "   Roberson R   "   ⎪
879066 "   Lynch. J.H   "   ⎪
860789 "   Thomas W.H   "   ⎪
861042 "   Wilson J   "   ⎭

2/Lt. J. Hodskin 18th Y & L
209696 Cpl McLean. W.S   "   ⎫
200804 L/Cpl Reaney G   "   ⎪
238096 Pte Pavelin. F   "   ⎪
62775   "   Watkinson G   "   ⎪
61961   "   Brewin. H   "   Hosp   ⎬ 18th. Y & L
53614   "   Childs G   "   ⎪   Section.
208605 "   Jones H   " Scarring leave 11/11/18
53604   "   Ash. J   "   ⎪
62239   "   France. F   "   ⎪
238100 "   Hilliard W   "   Hosp   ⎪
62078   "   Chapman. L.H   "   ⎪
208606 "   George O   "   ⎭
62462   "   Slack J   "   Company
62341   "   "
53683   "   Harper F   "
62423   "   Lamb F   "

H.Q. Section   80295 Pte Harris G   29 D.L.I
CAPT. E.K.B. PECK. 18th Y & L. 101669 A/Cpl Davis A.R. 29th. D.L.
238094 A/Sgt. Beer. H   "   205464 L/Cpl Acton J   "
02605 Pte Shaw. H   "   101664 Pte Collins W   "
879064   Hext (W) 33rd London Rgt. R.B. 101667 " Ferriss H.
860307 Pte Findlay J   "   85529   Smeer J
860789   Edwards J.T   "   100??   ????? J
860746   Green C.H   "   85514   Barrett J.H
861092   Wilson H   "   204032   Jarrett W.S
53682   Harper. F 18th Y & L. 62423   Lamb J 18 Y & L
62452   Slack J   "   67779
62341   "   86062 Slater J   Hosp
                                44411 Oates J.G
                                86081?

CONFIDENTIAL.

WAR DIARY

- of -

41st LIGHT TRENCH MORTAR BATTERY.

From: 1st February, 1919.
To: 28th February, 1919.

VOLUME IX.

Army Form C. 2118.

WAR DIARY
or
INTELLIGENCE SUMMARY.
(Erase heading not required.)

41st LTMB

FEBRUARY 1919

Instructions regarding War Diaries and Intelligence Summaries are contained in F. S. Regs., Part II. and the Staff Manual respectively. Title pages will be prepared in manuscript.

Place	Date	Hour	Summary of Events and Information	Remarks and references to Appendices
TOURCOING	1st		Returned from leave to UK. Rfn OATES to 33rd LRRB.	Appx
"	2nd		Demobilised Rfn HEWLETT 33rd LRRB. Demobilised Rfn PRITCHARD 33rd LRRB.	Appx
	3rd		Recreation + Training. Rfn BENCE 33rd LRRB	Appx
	4th		"	Appx
	5th		Demobilised Pte WATKINSON 18th Y+L and Rfn ROBINSON 33rd LRRB.	Appx
	6th		" from 33rd LRRB. Sgt. ERSKINE HQ and Cpl SADLER.	Appx
	7th		Recreation Training.	Appx
	8th		"	Appx
	9th		Demobilised Pte HILLIARD W. 18th Y+L.	Appx
	10th		Capt E.K.B. PECK MC returned from leave to UK.	Appx
	11th		Pte HARPER 18th Y+L " " "	Appx
	12/14th		Recreation Training. Demobilised L/Cpl SAWYER 18th York	Appx
	15.+16th		"	Appx
	17th		All personnel of Battery returned to their units and from this date 41st LTMB	Appx
			ceased to exist as a separate unit.	Appx

Jan Dean Capt.
O.C. 41st Lt TMB